Grammar Test Prep

Usage • Parts of Speech • Spelling
Capitalization • Punctuation

**usage
parts of speech
spelling
capitalization
punctuation**

Written by
Linda Schwartz

The Learning Works, Inc.

The Learning Works

Illustrations: Bev Armstrong
Editing: Kimberley Clark
Text Design: Clark Editorial & Design
Cover Illustrator: Rick Grayson
Cover Photographer: Ian Shaw / Getty Images

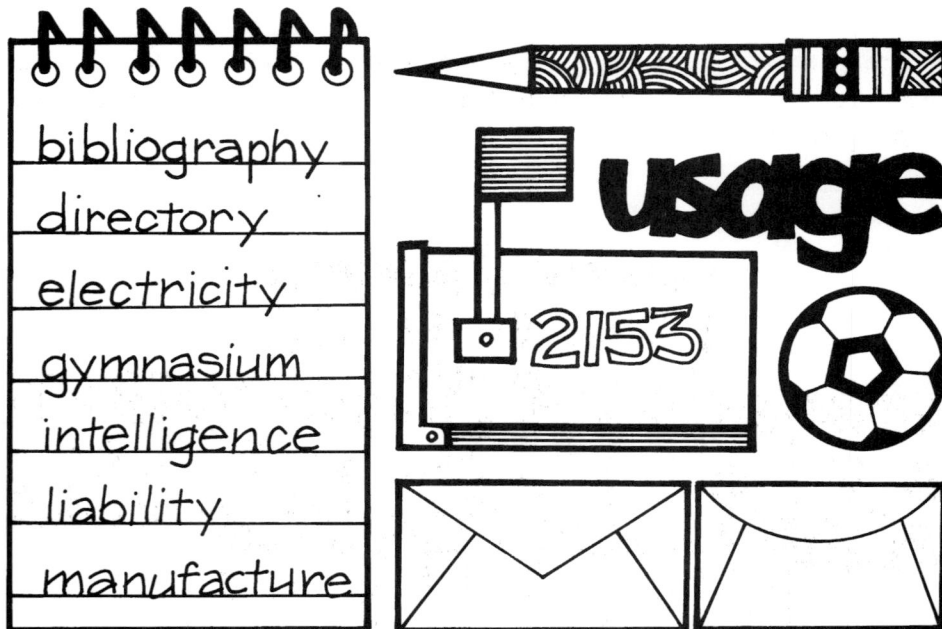

bibliography
directory
electricity
gymnasium
intelligence
liability
manufacture

usage

2153

Copyright © 2002
The Learning Works, Inc.

To the Teacher

The activities in this book were designed to help prepare students for the language portion of standardized tests. The book is divided into four main sections. The first section provides practice in usage and verb tenses. The second section gives students review in parts of speech. The third section contains spelling exercises, and the final section covers capitalization and punctuation.

In addition, you'll find basic rules of grammar, usage, subject–verb agreement, capitalization, and punctuation. These helpful "at-a-glance" rules can be reproduced for reference and review. Each page of rules has a border for easy identification.

For your convenience, there is a student record sheet to help you organize and keep track of your students' work. You'll also find a percentage table for easy grading. A reproducible "bubble" answer sheet is provided to give students practice in this test-taking skill.

Extend the practice activities by asking your students to make up similar exercises for classmates to solve. Students can make answer sheets to accompany their exercises.

usage
parts of speech
spelling
capitalization
punctuation

Contents

Bubble Answer Sheet 6

Record Sheet 7

Percentage Table 8

Usage • 9–18

Principal Parts of Verbs 10

Practice #1 11

Practice #2 12

Practice #3 13

Practice #4 14

Practice #5 15

Practice #6 16

Practice #7 17

Practice #8 18

Parts of Speech • 19–32

Nouns 20

Pronouns 21

Verbs 22

Review of Nouns, Pronouns, and Verbs 23

Rules for Subject–Verb Agreement 24

Subject–Verb Agreement 25

Adjectives 26

Adverbs 27

Parts of Speech Review #1 28

Prepositions 29

Conjunctions and Interjections 30

Parts of Speech Review #2 31

Parts of Speech Review #3 32

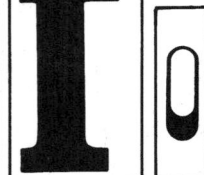

Contents

Spelling • 33–40

Tricky Words 34
Spelling Plurals #1 35
Spelling Plurals #2 36
Spelling Practice #1 37
Spelling Practice #2 38
Spelling Practice #3 39
Spelling Practice #4 40

Capitalization and Punctuation • 41–52

Rules of Capitalization 42
Capitalization Practice #1 43
Capitalization Practice #2 44
Capitalization Practice #3 45
Rules of Punctuation 46–47
Punctuation Practice #1 48
Punctuation Practice #2 49
Punctuation Practice #3 50
Final Review 51–52

Answer Key 53–56

Grammar Test Prep
© The Learning Works, Inc.

Bubble Answer Sheet

A Note to Students:

The number of questions varies depending on the activity.
Fill in the bubbles that are needed for each practice sheet you are assigned.

1. (a)
   (b)
   (c)
   (d)

2. (a)
   (b)
   (c)
   (d)

3. (a)
   (b)
   (c)
   (d)

4. (a)
   (b)
   (c)
   (d)

5. (a)
   (b)
   (c)
   (d)

6. (a)
   (b)
   (c)
   (d)

7. (a)
   (b)
   (c)
   (d)

8. (a)
   (b)
   (c)
   (d)

9. (a)
   (b)
   (c)
   (d)

10. (a)
    (b)
    (c)
    (d)

11. (a)
    (b)
    (c)
    (d)

12. (a)
    (b)
    (c)
    (d)

Record Sheet

	Page Number(s) of Activity	Number of Possible Answers	Number of Correct Answers	Percent Score
USAGE	11	12		
	12	12		
	13	12		
	14	12		
	15	12		
	16	12		
	17	12		
	18	12		
PARTS OF SPEECH	20	12		
	21	12		
	22	10		
	23	6		
	25	6		
	26	12		
	27	6		
	28	12		
	29	5		
	30	10		
	31	12		
	32	12		
SPELLING	35	12		
	36	12		
	37	12		
	38	12		
	39	10		
	40	10		
CAPITALIZATION AND PUNCTUATION	43	6		
	44	6		
	45	6		
	48	12		
	49	6		
	50	6		
	51–52	12		

Percentage Table

Number of Possible Answers	Number of Correct Answers											
	1	2	3	4	5	6	7	8	9	10	11	12
1	100											
2	50	100										
3	33	67	100									
4	25	50	75	100								
5	20	40	60	80	100							
6	17	33	50	67	83	100						
7	14	29	43	57	71	86	100					
8	13	25	38	50	63	75	88	100				
9	11	22	33	44	56	67	78	89	100			
10	10	20	30	40	50	60	70	80	90	100		
11	9	18	27	36	45	55	64	73	82	91	100	
12	8	17	25	33	42	50	58	67	75	83	92	100

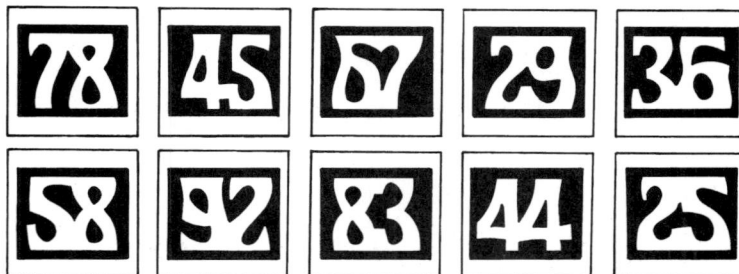

78 45 67 29 36

58 92 83 44 25

| you'll hike |
| pie tasted |
| I had fled |

Section 1: Usage

| Ed may win |
| bat cracked |
| I will climb |
| skate should |
| gem was lost |
| Amy pitches |
| chariot flew |

Principal Parts of Verbs

There are three principal parts of a verb: the infinitive or base form, the past-tense form, and the past participle. Most verbs form the past tense and past participle by adding *ed* to the base form. *Example: look–looked–looked*

Here is a list of some verbs that have irregular past-tense and past-participle forms.

Infinitive (base)	Past Tense	Past Participle
be	was, were	been
begin	began	begun
bite	bit	bitten
break	broke	broken
bring	brought	brought
choose	chose	chosen
come	came	come
do	did	done
draw	drew	drawn
drive	drove	driven
eat	ate	eaten
fall	fell	fallen
fly	flew	flown
forget	forgot	forgotten
freeze	froze	frozen
give	gave	given
go	went	gone
grow	grew	grown
hear	heard	heard
know	knew	known
lay	laid	laid
lie	lay	lain
lose	lost	lost
ring	rang	rung
rise	rose	risen
see	saw	seen
shake	shook	shaken
sit	sat	sat
speak	spoke	spoken
spring	sprang	sprung
steal	stole	stolen
swim	swam	swum
take	took	taken
tear	tore	torn
throw	threw	thrown
wear	wore	worn
write	wrote	written

Usage – Practice #1

Directions: Decide which word (or words) best completes each sentence.
On the answer sheet, fill in the bubble that corresponds to the correct answer.

1. I _____ most of the people at the party.
   a. knewed
   b. known
   c. knew
   d. knowed

2. That was the _____ movie I have ever seen.
   a. best
   b. better
   c. bestest
   d. goodest

3. Jeffrey is the _____ of the two boys.
   a. oldest
   b. most old
   c. more older
   d. older

4. I completely _____ about our soccer practice.
   a. forget
   b. forgotten
   c. forgot
   d. have forgotten

5. Dad has _____ a letter to the editor.
   a. wrote
   b. write
   c. wroten
   d. written

6. We _____ in the lake yesterday.
   a. swam
   b. swimmed
   c. swum
   d. swammed

7. Please _____ me for your team.
   a. chose
   b. choose
   c. chosen
   d. chosed

8. I have never _____ anything like it!
   a. saw
   b. see
   c. seed
   d. seen

9. The pond was _____, so we went skating.
   a. freeze
   b. froze
   c. frozed
   d. frozen

10. We _____ at the new restaurant last night.
    a. ate
    b. eat
    c. have eaten
    d. eaten

11. He had been _____ a new locker at school.
    a. gave
    b. gaven
    c. given
    d. give

12. It is our turn to _____ the carpool.
    a. drove
    b. drive
    c. driven
    d. have driven

number correct _____

percentage _____

Name _____

Usage – Practice #2

Directions: Decide which word (or words) best completes each sentence.
On the answer sheet, fill in the bubble that corresponds to the correct answer.

1. Mom and I _____ going shopping.
   a. is
   b. wasn't
   c. was
   d. are

2. Our teacher gave _____ extra time for reading.
   a. themselves
   b. us
   c. our
   d. we

3. Last night I _____ of an idea for my science fair project.
   a. thinked
   b. have thought
   c. thought
   d. thinks

4. I have never _____ on a train.
   a. rode
   b. ride
   c. rides
   d. ridden

5. My baby sister has _____ the car keys.
   a. hide
   b. hiding
   c. hidden
   d. hid

6. Yesterday my family _____ to Miami.
   a. flew
   b. fly
   c. flown
   d. have flown

7. I hope she will _____ me a letter.
   a. wrote
   b. write
   c. written
   d. writing

8. When the bell _____, recess was over.
   a. rung
   b. ring
   c. have rung
   d. rang

9. I must _____ to her about her report.
   a. speak
   b. spoke
   c. spoken
   d. speaking

10. New classes have _____ this fall.
    a. begin
    b. began
    c. begins
    d. begun

11. They have _____ a new president.
    a. choose
    b. chosen
    c. chose
    d. choosing

12. What are you going to _____ to the game?
    a. wore
    b. wear
    c. worn
    d. wearing

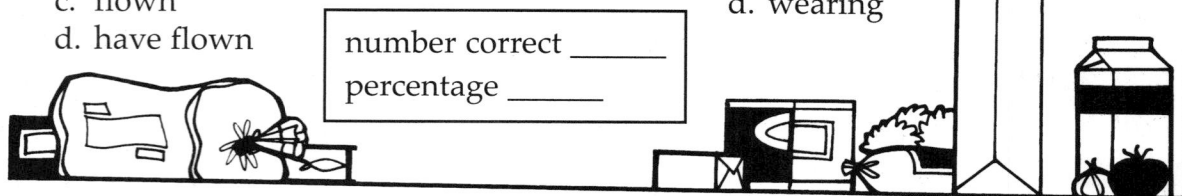

number correct _____

percentage _____

Usage – Practice #3

Directions: Decide which word (or words) best completes each sentence.
On the answer sheet, fill in the bubble that corresponds to the correct answer.

1. This is the _____ report card I have ever had.
   a. better
   b. best
   c. good
   d. goodest

2. My brother is _____ than me.
   a. tall
   b. taller
   c. tallest
   d. most tall

3. Yesterday's storm was the _____ of the season.
   a. bad
   b. baddest
   c. worse
   d. worst

4. This is a _____ book than the one I just read.
   a. better
   b. best
   c. good
   d. gooder

5. Jamal is the _____ runner on the team.
   a. fast
   b. fastly
   c. faster
   d. fastest

6. We _____ her at the office this morning.
   a. see
   b. seen
   c. saw
   d. had seen

7. I have never _____ on an airplane.
   a. fly
   b. flew
   c. flown
   d. flied

8. José has _____ an essay for the contest.
   a. write
   b. written
   c. wrote
   d. writes

9. Grandma has _____ her for six years.
   a. knew
   b. know
   c. known
   d. knowed

10. She _____ the ball to third base.
    a. threw
    b. throw
    c. thrown
    d. have thrown

11. Have you _____ out the garbage?
    a. take
    b. took
    c. tooken
    d. taken

12. He _____ the Los Angeles Marathon.
    a. ran
    b. run
    c. runned
    d. have run

number correct _____
percentage _____

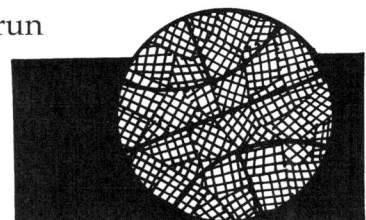

Grammar Test Prep
© The Learning Works, Inc.

Name _____

Usage – Practice #4

Directions: Decide which word (or words) best completes each sentence.
On the answer sheet, fill in the bubble that corresponds to the correct answer.

1. The guest speaker showed _____ a slide show.
   a. myself
   b. we
   c. us
   d. themselves

2. One of the girls _____ riding with us.
   a. are
   b. is
   c. were
   d. has

3. _____ both of these books yours?
   a. Is
   b. Has
   c. Are
   d. Was

4. Anyone on the four teams _____ eligible to play.
   a. is
   b. are
   c. were
   d. have

5. Many members of my family _____ Spanish.
   a. speaks
   b. spoken
   c. has spoken
   d. speak

6. They have _____ work on the science fair project.
   a. begin
   b. begun
   c. began
   d. beginned

7. She was the first person _____ for the team.
   a. choose
   b. chose
   c. choosed
   d. chosen

8. My friends _____ to see me in the play.
   a. came
   b. come
   c. has come
   d. comed

9. They have already _____ to catch the bus.
   a. go
   b. went
   c. gone
   d. goes

10. My younger sister has _____ up so quickly.
    a. grow
    b. grown
    c. grew
    d. grewed

11. The bell _____ for recess.
    a. ring
    b. ringed
    c. rang
    d. rung

12. The building _____ when the quake hit.
    a. shake
    b. shaken
    c. shooked
    d. shook

| number correct _____ |
| percentage _____ |

Name _____

Usage – Practice #5

Directions: Decide which word (or words) best completes each sentence.
On the answer sheet, fill in the bubble that corresponds to the correct answer.

1. He has _____ the same socks for four days.
   a. wear
   b. wears
   c. wore
   d. worn

2. _____ those old shoes away!
   a. Throw
   b. Threw
   c. Throws
   d. Thrown

3. Mom _____ the lettuce into small pieces.
   a. tear
   b. tore
   c. have torn
   d. torn

4. Rain has _____ for six days in a row.
   a. fall
   b. fell
   c. fallen
   d. falls

5. We _____ up and headed for home.
   a. gave
   b. give
   c. has given
   d. given

6. I have _____ his last name.
   a. forget
   b. forgets
   c. forgot
   d. forgotten

7. The puppy _____ my finger.
   a. bit
   b. bite
   c. bitted
   d. bitten

8. The sun will _____ at 6:00 A.M. tomorrow.
   a. rise
   b. rose
   c. risen
   d. rised

9. I _____ too much at dinner.
   a. eats
   b. ate
   c. eaten
   d. has eaten

10. Do you _____ how to solve this problem?
    a. knew
    b. know
    c. knows
    d. known

11. We could have _____ if we tried harder.
    a. win
    b. wins
    c. winned
    d. won

12. She _____ me to a rock concert.
    a. take
    b. taken
    c. took
    d. have taken

| number correct _____ |
| percentage _____ |

Grammar Test Prep
© The Learning Works, Inc.

Name _____

Usage – Practice #6

Directions: Decide which word (or words) best completes each sentence.
On the answer sheet, fill in the bubble that corresponds to the correct answer.

1. The t-shirt _____ in the dryer.
   a. shrink
   b. shrank
   c. shrunk
   d. have shrunk

2. He _____ and sprained his ankle.
   a. fall
   b. falls
   c. fell
   d. fallen

3. We _____ the game by three points.
   a. lost
   b. losted
   c. losed
   d. lose

4. We have already _____ the course twice.
   a. ran
   b. ranned
   c. run
   d. running

5. Jeff and _____ are going swimming later.
   a. me
   b. I
   c. him
   d. myself

6. Pears and bananas _____ my favorite fruits.
   a. is
   b. am
   c. are
   d. was

7. _____ leaving in the morning.
   a. We've
   b. We'll
   c. Weren't
   d. We're

8. The runner _____ second base.
   a. steal
   b. stolen
   c. have stolen
   d. stole

9. We left _____ than the first group.
   a. late
   b. later
   c. latest
   d. lately

10. He _____ a suit to graduation.
    a. wear
    b. wearing
    c. wore
    d. worn

11. We need to _____ a new employee.
    a. hire
    b. hires
    c. hired
    d. hiring

12. I don't think they _____ me.
    a. hears
    b. heard
    c. hearing
    d. herd

number correct _____

percentage _____

Name _____

Usage – Practice #7

Directions: Decide which word (or words) best completes each sentence.
On the answer sheet, fill in the bubble that corresponds to the correct answer.

1. She _____ in a very soft voice.
   a. speak
   b. speaks
   c. have spoken
   d. spoken

2. Let's _____ up the balloons up for the party.
   a. blew
   b. blews
   c. blow
   d. blown

3. Mom got to _____ first class to New York.
   a. fly
   b. flew
   c. flown
   d. have flown

4. Give the books to _____ for the review.
   a. they
   b. their
   c. there
   d. them

5. Yesterday we _____ in my brother's new car.
   a. ride
   b. rides
   c. rode
   d. have ridden

6. When do your piano lessons _____?
   a. begin
   b. began
   c. begun
   d. beginned

7. The baby _____ all night long.
   a. cry
   b. cried
   c. crying
   d. have cried

8. _____ were the spelling champs this year.
   a. Their
   b. There
   c. Them
   d. They

9. Dave _____ me his backpack to hold.
   a. give
   b. have given
   c. gave
   d. giving

10. How long have you _____ her?
    a. knew
    b. know
    c. knows
    d. known

11. I _____ the shortcut to school every day.
    a. take
    b. takes
    c. taken
    d. has taken

12. One of the players _____ injured.
    a. were
    b. was
    c. are
    d. being

number correct _____

percentage _____

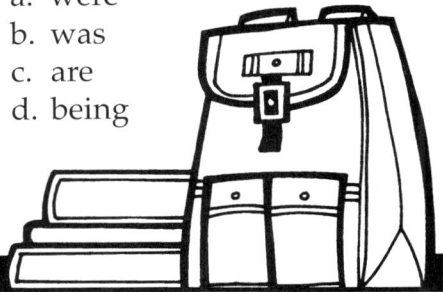

Name _____

Usage – Practice #8

Directions: Decide which word (or words) best completes each sentence.
On the answer sheet, fill in the bubble that corresponds to the correct answer.

1. Please give the book to _____.
    a. his
    b. I
    c. me
    d. myself

2. Two of my classmates _____ absent.
    a. is
    b. are
    c. be
    d. being

3. _____ the application come in the mail yet?
    a. Are
    b. Is
    c. Has
    d. Have

4. Each of the players _____ qualified.
    a. seem
    b. seems
    c. seams
    d. have seen

5. Many in the world _____ hungry every day.
    a. going
    b. goes
    c. go
    d. has gone

6. _____ several teachers going to the convention?
    a. Is
    b. Are
    c. Was
    d. Has

7. I plan to bring _____ to the grand opening.
    a. they
    b. their
    c. we
    d. them

8. Is that message for _____?
    a. I
    b. she
    c. me
    d. they

9. _____ were asked to be on the student council.
    a. Us
    b. Him
    c. She
    d. We

10. You and _____ sit over here next to me.
    a. she
    b. hers
    c. her
    d. them

11. Did you invite _____ to join us?
    a. they
    b. them
    c. they're
    d. their

12. Wendy sent the package to _____.
    a. we
    b. they
    c. me
    d. I

| number correct _____ |
| percentage _____ |

Section 2:
Parts of Speech

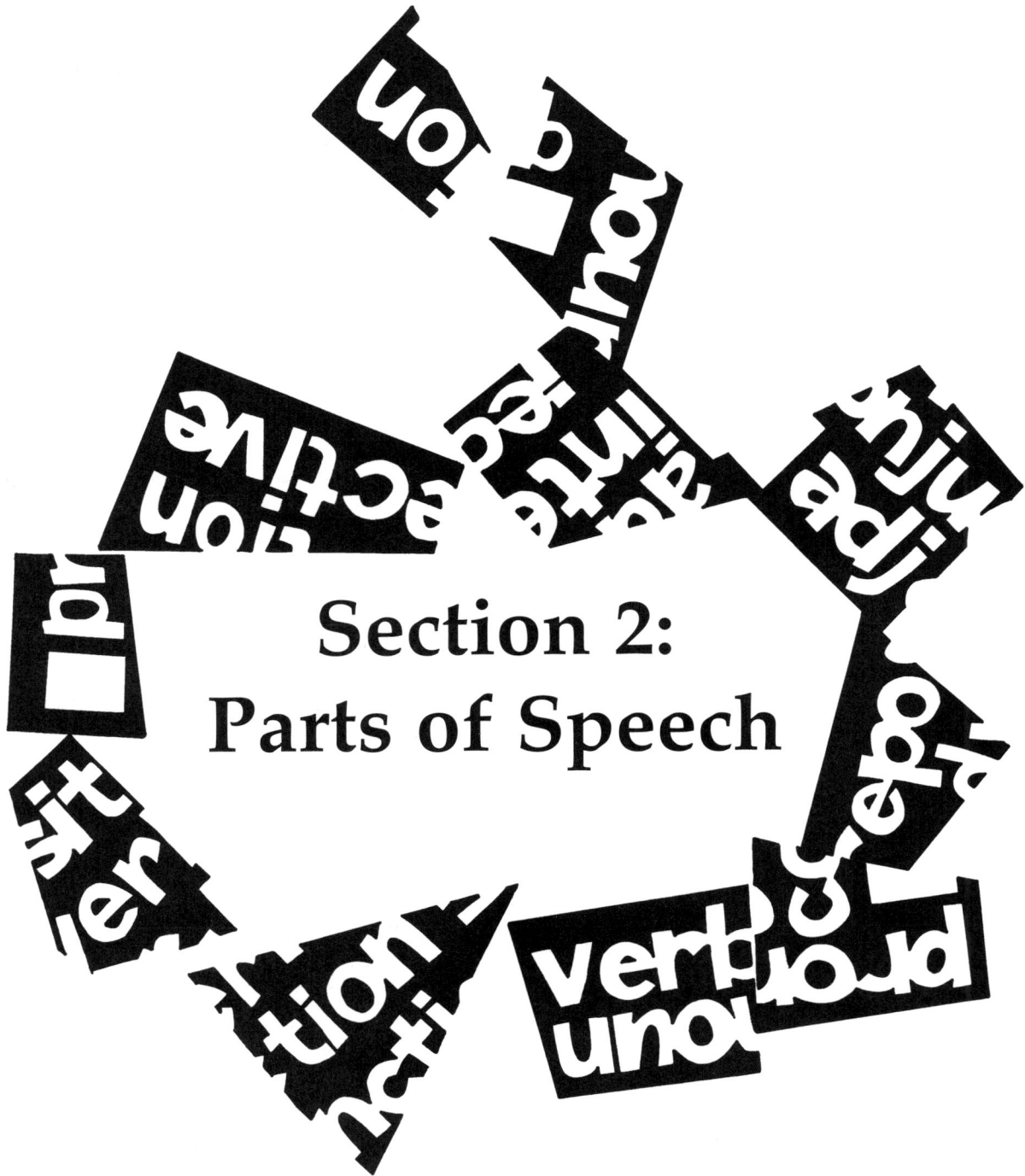

Name _____

Nouns

> A **noun** is the name of a person, place, thing, quality, or ideal.

Directions: Find the noun or nouns in each sentence below.
On the answer sheet, fill in the bubble that corresponds to the correct answer.

1. My dog wagged her tail when she saw me.
   a. My, dog, tail
   b. dog, tail
   c. dog, tail, me
   d. My, dog, tail, she, me

2. The girl sitting by the window is our class president.
   a. window, class, president
   b. girl, president
   c. girl, sitting, window, class
   d. girl, window, president

3. My family lives in Lodi, California.
   a. My, family, California
   b. family, Lodi
   c. family, Lodi, California
   d. family, lives, Lodi, California

4. Our picnic was a success except for all the ants.
   a. Our, picnic, ants
   b. Our, picnic, except, ants
   c. picnic, success, all, ants
   d. picnic, success, ants

5. The elderly man sitting on the park bench is my grandfather.
   a. man, bench, grandfather
   b. elderly, man, park, grandfather
   c. man, park, grandfather
   d. man, park, bench, grandfather

6. My brother and sister are arriving on the afternoon plane.
   a. my, brother, sister, afternoon
   b. brother, sister, arriving, afternoon
   c. brother, sister, plane
   d. brother, sister, afternoon, plane

7. I hope she comes to my soccer game.
   a. I, hope, she, soccer
   b. she, soccer
   c. game
   d. she, soccer, game

8. Dad bought me the cutest puppy.
   a. Dad, puppy
   b. bought, puppy
   c. Dad, cutest, puppy
   d. Dad, bought, puppy

9. I love snow but don't like shoveling it.
   a. I, snow, shoveling
   b. love, like
   c. snow, shoveling, it
   d. snow

10. I exercise before school each day.
    a. I, exercise, school
    b. exercise, day
    c. school, day
    d. school

11. The blaring sirens kept me awake all night.
    a. sirens
    b. sirens, night
    c. blaring, sirens, all, night
    d. sirens, awake, night

12. Who ate the chocolate chip cookies?
    a. Who, chip, cookies
    b. Who, cookies
    c. chocolate, chip, cookies
    d. cookies

number correct _____
percentage _____

Name _____

Pronouns

> A **pronoun** is a word used in place of a noun. A pronoun may stand for the name of a person, place, thing, quality, or ideal.

Directions: In each group of words, find the one that is **not** a pronoun.
On the answer sheet, fill in the bubble that corresponds to the correct answer.

1. a. you
    b. us
    c. mom
    d. them

2. a. I
    b. man
    c. she
    d. they

3. a. it
    b. their
    c. me
    d. there

4. a. self
    b. your
    c. their
    d. each

5. a. himself
    b. mine
    c. ours
    d. hours

6. a. myself
    b. body
    c. herself
    d. he

7. a. no
    b. anybody
    c. nobody
    d. no one

8. a. herself
    b. either
    c. about
    d. both

9. a. neither
    b. away
    c. itself
    d. her

10. a. all
    b. ourselves
    c. yourself
    d. at

11. a. with
    b. any
    c. both
    d. somebody

12. a. few
    b. until
    c. everybody
    d. anyone

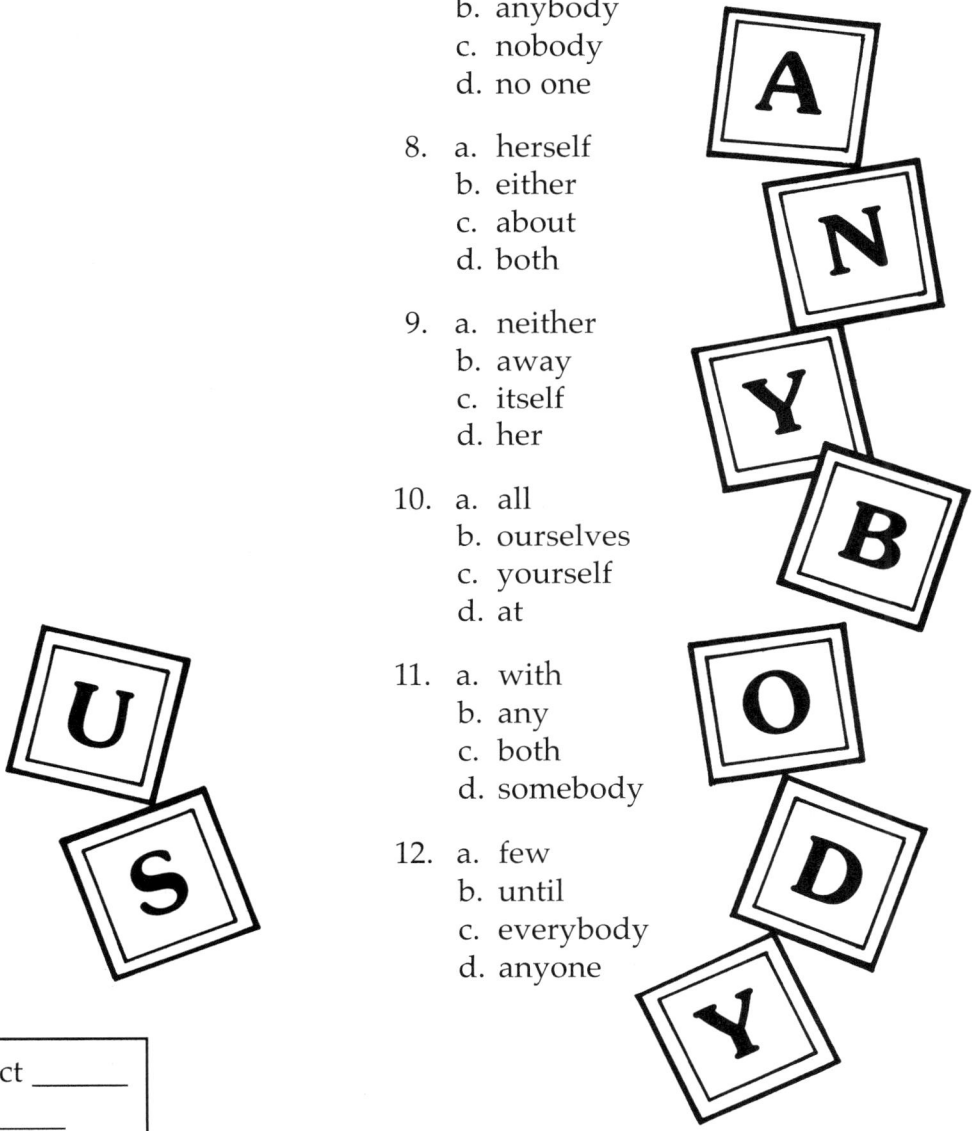

number correct _____
percentage _____

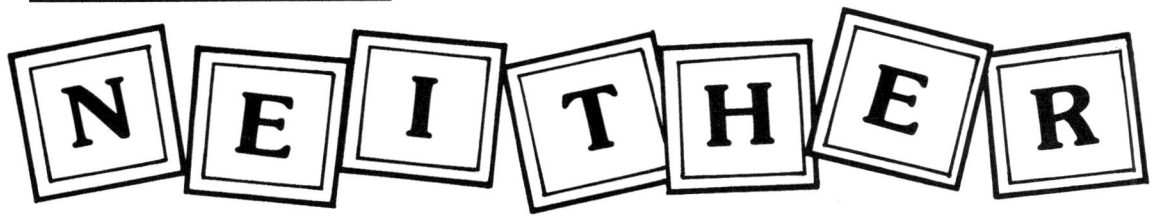

Name _____

Verbs

A **verb** is a word that expresses an act, occurrence, or state of being. A sentence may have a main verb and one or more **auxiliary**, or helping verbs. Here is a list of auxiliary, or helping verbs:

am	be	had	shall	may
is	being	do	will	might
are	been	does	should	must
was	has	did	would	can
were	have			could

Directions: Find the verb or verbs in each sentence.
On the answer sheet, fill in the bubble that corresponds to the correct answer.

1. I cut the pattern and glued it to my paper.
   a. cut
   b. cut, pattern
   c. glued
   d. cut, glued

2. We drove for a few hours and stopped for lunch.
   a. drove
   b. drove, few
   c. drove, stopped
   d. stopped, lunch

3. He is my best friend.
   a. He, is, friend
   b. He, is
   c. is
   d. is, my, friend

4. She has not been feeling well lately.
   a. has, been, feeling
   b. She, has, not, been, feeling
   c. She, has, been, feeling
   d. feeling, well

5. I have given her my notes to study.
   a. I, have, study
   b. have, given
   c. have, given, study
   d. have, my, study

6. We must leave immediately.
   a. We
   b. must, immediately
   c. leave
   d. must, leave

7. They have had six days of rain.
   a. They, had
   b. have, had
   c. had
   d. had, rain

8. Will you pass the bottle of mustard?
   a. pass
   b. Will, pass
   c. pass, mustard
   d. pass, bottle

9. Where have you been hiding all this time?
   a. Where, been
   b. been, hiding
   c. have, been, hiding
   d. have, hiding

10. Do you know the answer to the question?
    a. Do
    b. Do, know
    c. Do, know, answer
    d. know, question

number correct _____

percentage _____

Name _____

Review of Nouns, Pronouns, and Verbs

Directions: In each group of sentences, find the sentence with an error.
Fill in the bubble on the answer sheet that corresponds to the incorrect sentence.

1. a. Our neighbor's lawn was overgrown with weeds.
    b. The baby's toys were scattered all over the floor.
    c. The player's uniforms got drenched when it started to pour during the game.
    d. Michael's backpack was filled with supplies for his hike.

2. a. It's hot and muggy outside.
    b. It's not too early to apply for the summer program.
    c. He hasn't been by to see us in a long time.
    d. My dog lost it's tag during our afternoon walk.

3. a. My brother and I saw a great movie this weekend.
    b. Randy asked Paul and I to go fishing with him.
    c. Dad drove us to the library so we could do research for our social studies project.
    d. The boys rode their bikes over there yesterday.

4. a. Susan gave Carol and me part of her sandwich.
    b. Everyone said that he and I did a good job painting the fence.
    c. Is that telephone call for him or me?
    d. Mom divided the cookies between my sister and I.

5. a. Childrens' clothing will go on sale next week.
    b. The student's pencil broke during the exam.
    c. The woman's purse was stolen while she was shopping.
    d. One of Linda's books is missing.

6. a. How was the rock concert?
    b. You and him did a great job on the science project.
    c. Hannah brought Stan and me a pizza for dinner.
    d. We were not home when she came to visit, so she left us a note.

number correct _____
percentage _____

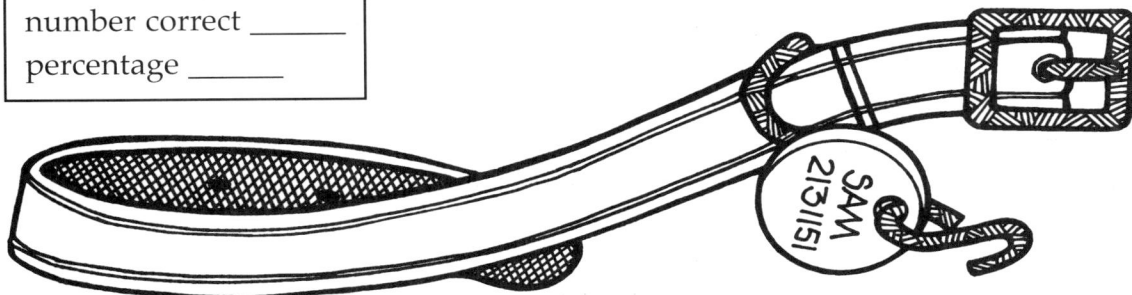

Rules for Subject–Verb Agreement

- A singular subject takes a singular verb.

    *Example: The <u>cat</u> **is** asleep.*

- A plural subject takes a plural verb.

    *Example: The <u>cats</u> **are** asleep.*

- There are a few exceptions to the rules above. Some nouns that are plural in form take a singular verb.

    *Examples: <u>News</u> **travels** fast around here.*

    *<u>Economics</u> **is** taught at the local junior college.*

- If the subject of the verb is made up of two or more words joined by **and**, the verb is plural. However, if the words are thought of as one unit, a singular verb is used.

    *Examples: <u>Potatoes and corn</u> **are** my favorite vegetables.*

    *<u>Bread and butter</u> **is** served with breakfast.*

- If the subject consists of two or more words joined by the words **or** or **nor**, the verb should agree with the subject that follows **or** or **nor**.

    *Examples: Either <u>Jessie **or** the two boys</u> **come** here after school each day.*

    *Neither <u>the doctor **nor** one</u> of her nurses **is** available.*

- A noun that indicates a space of time, an amount of money, or a unit of measurement takes a singular verb even when the form is plural.

    Examples: (space of time)

    *<u>Three weeks</u> **is** not enough time to see all of Canada.*

    (amount of money)

    *<u>Fifty-five cents</u> **is** not a lot of money for this used paperback book.*

    (unit of measurement)

    *<u>Five miles</u> **is** a long way to run.*

- When a phrase comes between the subject and the verb, you should still look at the subject to determine the form of the verb.

    *Examples: <u>One</u> of the gifts **is** missing.*

    *<u>Four</u> of the puppies **are** already sold.*

Name _____

Subject–Verb Agreement

Directions: In each sentence below, underline the simple subject and predicate. Find the sentence where the subject and verb are **not** in agreement. On the answer sheet, fill in the bubble that corresponds to the letter of the incorrect sentence.

1. a. There is scores of teenagers at the football game tonight.
   b. All of us were planning to attend the fair.
   c. A few miles down the road stands an old farmhouse.
   d. Several of the girls in my homeroom were in the play.

2. a. They are on their way.
   b. Of all the players on the team, Raul is the fastest.
   c. One of the students in our class sing in the show.
   d. Four of us are planning to travel to Europe this summer.

3. a. The dog and cat were constantly fighting.
   b. The committee of student council officers has voted to approve the school dance.
   c. Either the professor or one of her assistants attend the banquet every year.
   d. Mathematics is taught in second, third, and fifth periods only.

4. a. Twenty-four dollars are the price of his latest best-selling book.
   b. Peanut butter and jelly is still my favorite sandwich.
   c. Henry, Ed, and José plan to be at the party.
   d. Cheese and milk are good sources of calcium.

5. a. The members of the committee will meet this evening.
   b. Most electrical engineers earn good salaries.
   c. One of the excuses given by the student was that the dog ate her homework.
   d. Neither Jan nor the twins expects to be home tonight.

6. a. The rules of the game are easy to understand.
   b. The news about the earthquake is not good.
   c. One of the members of the band have the measles.
   d. Both of us were surprised to hear the story.

| number correct _____ |
| percentage _____ |

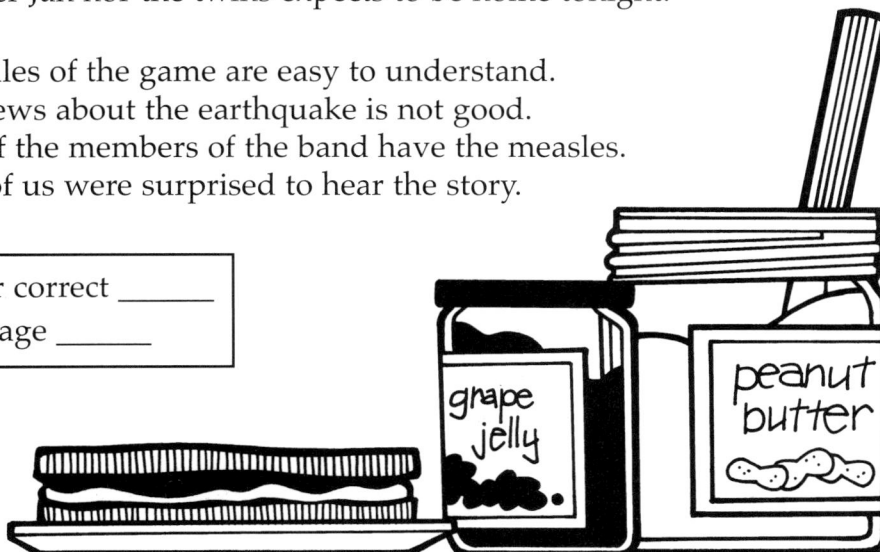

Name _____

Adjectives

> An **adjective** is a word that describes a noun or a pronoun.
> An adjective tells how many, what kind, or which one.

Directions: In each group of words, find the underlined word that is **not** an adjective. On the answer sheet, fill in the bubble that corresponds to the correct answer.

1. a. <u>wonderful</u> party
    b. stopped <u>suddenly</u>
    c. <u>juicy</u> pear
    d. <u>yellow</u> jacket

2. a. <u>unusual</u> painting
    b. <u>ancient</u> artifact
    c. <u>loose</u> tooth
    d. leaving <u>shortly</u>

3. a. <u>jubilant</u> crowd
    b. <u>queasy</u> stomach
    c. <u>choir</u> singing
    d. <u>lovely</u> sunset

4. a. <u>deceptively</u> easy
    b. <u>enormous</u> skyscraper
    c. <u>delightful</u> person
    d. <u>gentle</u> animal

5. a. <u>single</u> line
    b. <u>signal</u> them
    c. <u>silky</u> material
    d. <u>three</u> wishes

6. a. <u>vivid</u> imagination
    b. <u>eligible</u> voter
    c. <u>obscure</u> idea
    d. arrive <u>tomorrow</u>

7. a. <u>carefully</u> placed
    b. <u>six</u> guests
    c. <u>tallest</u> player
    d. <u>that</u> notebook

8. a. <u>purple</u> raincoat
    b. <u>sweltering</u> heat
    c. <u>crawled</u> up
    d. <u>ripest</u> peach

9. a. <u>family</u> vacation
    b. <u>crazy</u> idea
    c. <u>last</u> Wednesday
    d. <u>slowly</u> began

10. a. <u>American</u> flag
    b. <u>antique</u> car
    c. <u>patiently</u> explained
    d. <u>sandy</u> beach

11. a. <u>fluffy</u> kitten
    b. <u>eighth</u> grade
    c. <u>picket</u> fence
    d. <u>in</u> Nashville

12. a. <u>sang</u> beautifully
    b. <u>chocolate</u> cupcakes
    c. <u>hilarious</u> joke
    d. <u>diamond</u> ring

number correct _____
percentage _____

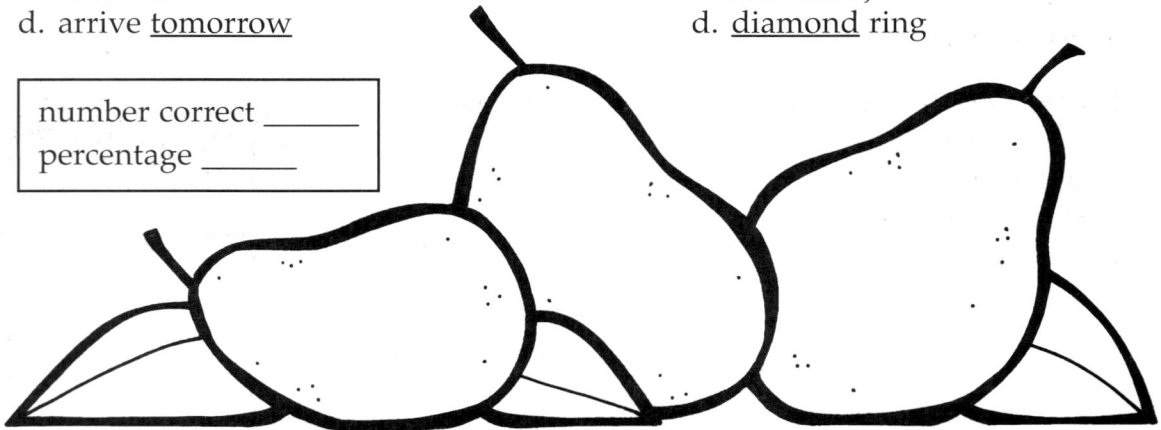

Name _____

Adverbs

An **adverb** is a word that describes a verb, an adjective, or another adverb. An adverb tells how, when, where, how often, or to what degree.

Directions: Find the adverb or adverbs in each sentence below.
On the answer sheet, fill in the bubble that corresponds to the correct answer.

1. The instructions clearly tell you to add four teaspoons of flour.
   a. instructions
   b. clearly
   c. clearly, tell
   d. four

2. Yesterday I waited patiently for the mail carrier to deliver my acceptance letter.
   a. waited, patiently
   b. Yesterday
   c. Yesterday, acceptance
   d. Yesterday, patiently

3. We were there when the suspect suddenly appeared.
   a. were
   b. suspect, appeared
   c. there
   d. there, suddenly

4. It is almost impossible to do this task quickly.
   a. It, impossible
   b. almost, task
   c. almost, quickly
   d. almost

5. Soon it will be time for us to leave this house forever.
   a. Soon, forever
   b. it, forever
   c. time, forever
   d. Soon, leave

6. The weather was extremely hot, so we went inside.
   a. was, went
   b. hot, inside
   c. extremely, inside
   d. extremely

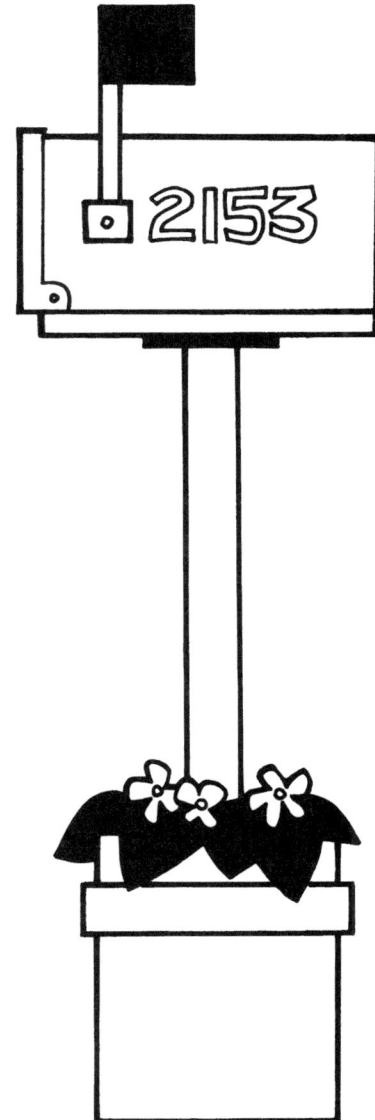

number correct _____
percentage _____

Name _____

Parts of Speech Review #1

Directions: What parts of speech are the underlined words in the sentences below?
On the answer sheet, fill in the bubble that corresponds to the correct answer.

1. The beetle <u>scampered</u> under the <u>couch</u>.
   a. noun – verb
   b. verb – verb
   c. verb – noun
   d. adverb – noun

2. We're <u>going</u> to the <u>baseball</u> game.
   a. noun – noun
   b. pronoun – noun
   c. verb – adverb
   d. verb – adjective

3. I ate <u>too</u> much at dinner.
   a. noun – adjective
   b. pronoun – noun
   c. verb – adverb
   d. pronoun – adverb

4. <u>Emily</u> is a great <u>math</u> student.
   a. noun – adjective
   b. noun – noun
   c. pronoun – noun
   d. noun – adverb

5. It doesn't <u>matter</u> if you don't win as long as you give it your <u>best</u>.
   a. verb – noun
   b. adverb – noun
   c. noun – adjective
   d. verb – adverb

6. <u>He</u> learned an <u>important</u> lesson.
   a. verb – noun
   b. pronoun – adjective
   c. pronoun – verb
   d. noun – adjective

7. <u>Three</u> kids piled into the <u>back</u> seat.
   a. noun – noun
   b. adverb – adjective
   c. adjective – adjective
   d. adverb – noun

8. I <u>would</u> <u>like</u> you to be on my committee.
   a. noun – verb
   b. verb – verb
   c. adjective – verb
   d. verb – adverb

9. <u>Put</u> my books over <u>there</u>.
   a. verb – noun
   b. verb – adjective
   c. verb – adverb
   d. adverb – adverb

10. This is the <u>same</u> book I read <u>earlier</u>.
    a. noun – adjective
    b. pronoun – adverb
    c. adverb – adverb
    d. adjective – adverb

11. The boy in the <u>blue</u> jacket is my <u>cousin</u>.
    a. noun – noun
    b. noun – pronoun
    c. adjective – noun
    d. adverb – noun

12. <u>His</u> sister is my <u>best</u> friend.
    a. noun – adjective
    b. pronoun – adjective
    c. verb – adverb
    d. adverb – adjective

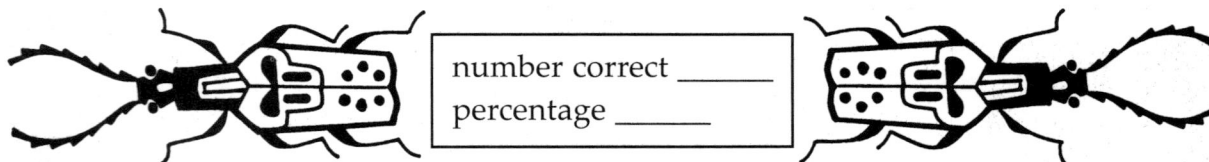

number correct _____
percentage _____

Name _____

Prepositions

> A **preposition** is a word that can be combined with a noun or pronoun to form a phrase that tells something about some other part of a sentence.
> This group of words is called a <u>prepositional phrase</u>.
> *Examples: The plane flew **above** <u>the clouds</u>.*
> *The actors stood **behind** <u>the curtains</u>.*

Directions: In the sentences below, the prepositions should be in **bold** type and the <u>prepositional phrases</u> should be underlined. In each group, find the one sentence that is **not** marked correctly. On the answer sheet, fill in the bubble that corresponds to the incorrectly marked sentence.

1. a. **During** <u>the storm</u>, the boat headed **for** <u>the harbor</u>.
    b. She read a book **in** <u>the library</u>.
    c. **Over** <u>the years</u>, we have visited **many** <u>foreign countries</u> around the world.
    d. The horse trotted **toward** <u>the barn</u> when his owner called.

2. a. The teenager sat **behind** <u>the wheel</u> ready **for** <u>her driving test</u>.
    b. The man walked **along** <u>the road</u> hoping someone would give him a ride.
    c. The doctor strode **into** <u>the room</u> and delivered the good news **to** <u>her patient</u>.
    d. Between you and me, I think she should go **before** <u>it gets dark</u>.

3. a. **Throughout** <u>the world</u>, people are hoping for peace and tolerance among nations.
    b. **On** <u>Thanksgiving morning</u>, we all sat **around** <u>the table</u> talking and laughing.
    c. The dog found her bone hidden **under** <u>the blanket</u>.
    d. **After** <u>the game</u>, everyone went home tired and hoarse.

4. a. **Against** <u>all odds</u>, our soccer team was chosen the best **in** <u>the league</u>.
    b. Yesterday, Stephen **won** <u>the title</u> easily **without** <u>any problems</u>.
    c. The erratic fly ball hit him **on** <u>the head</u>.
    d. The girls went **across** <u>the street</u> to buy oranges **for** <u>dinner</u>.

5. a. **Before** <u>you sign</u>, you should read the document **very** <u>carefully</u>.
    b. The bird flew **in** <u>lazy circles</u> **above** <u>our heads</u>.
    c. Her house is **beyond** <u>the lake</u> and **around** <u>the next corner</u>.
    d. **Until** <u>they leave</u>, I can't start my homework or work **on** <u>my project</u>.

| number correct _____ |
| percentage _____ |

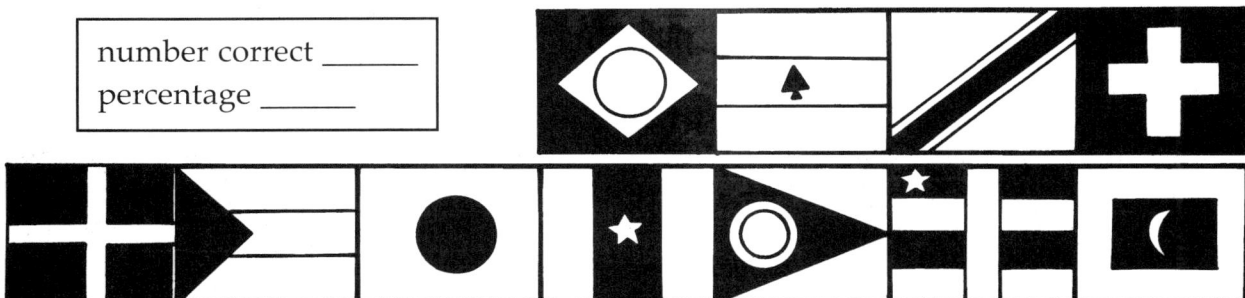

Grammar Test Prep
© The Learning Works, Inc.

Name _____

Conjunctions and Interjections

A **conjunction** is a word that joins together
individual words or groups of words in a sentence.

*Examples: coordinating conjunctions: and, but, for, nor, or
correlative conjunctions: either–or, neither–nor, not only–but also
subordinating conjunctions: after, as, because, if, since, when*

An **interjection** is a word that expresses emotion
and has no grammatical relation to other words in a sentence.

Examples: ah, alas, oh, ouch, ow, ugh, whew

Directions: What part of speech is the underlined word in each of the sentences below?
On the answer sheet, fill in the bubble that corresponds to the correct answer.

1. <u>Whew!</u> That was a heavy bookshelf to move!
   a. noun
   b. interjection
   c. conjunction
   d. preposition

2. I want to go, <u>but</u> I have to study for a final.
   a. verb
   b. adverb
   c. conjunction
   d. preposition

3. I have not <u>forgotten</u> my promise.
   a. verb
   b. pronoun
   c. adverb
   d. preposition

4. Juan got a job <u>after</u> school.
   a. noun
   b. pronoun
   c. adjective
   d. preposition

5. You can ride with me, <u>or</u> you can go with Risa.
   a. verb
   b. conjunction
   c. pronoun
   d. adverb

6. That folder is <u>mine</u>.
   a. noun
   b. pronoun
   c. conjunction
   d. preposition

7. <u>Oh!</u> What a pleasant surprise!
   a. verb
   b. adjective
   c. conjunction
   d. interjection

8. The heater is broken, <u>and</u> it's freezing in here.
   a. conjunction
   b. interjection
   c. verb
   d. preposition

9. <u>Someone</u> is knocking at the door.
   a. noun
   b. pronoun
   c. adjective
   d. adverb

10. The doctor said no jogging <u>or</u> soccer until my ankle heals.
    a. interjection
    b. adjective
    c. adverb
    d. conjunction

number correct _____

percentage _____

Name _____

Parts of Speech Review #2

Directions: What part of speech is the underlined word in each of the sentences below?
On the answer sheet, fill in the bubble that corresponds to the correct answer.

1. I want to go, <u>but</u> I have the flu.
   a. noun
   b. verb
   c. conjunction
   d. preposition

2. The ball rolled <u>under</u> the couch.
   a. verb
   b. adjective
   c. conjunction
   d. preposition

3. He <u>is</u> my best friend.
   a. noun
   b. pronoun
   c. verb
   d. preposition

4. Does Rick know that <u>he</u> is the winner?
   a. noun
   b. pronoun
   c. adjective
   d. adverb

5. The detective walked <u>cautiously</u> toward the house.
   a. verb
   b. adjective
   c. adverb
   d. pronoun

6. She has a <u>brilliant</u> mind.
   a. adjective
   b. adverb
   c. pronoun
   d. preposition

7. What <u>advice</u> can you give me?
   a. noun
   b. verb
   c. adjective
   d. adverb

8. I would <u>advise</u> you to talk to your teacher about the assignment.
   a. noun
   b. verb
   c. adjective
   d. preposition

9. Please come <u>here</u> immediately.
   a. noun
   b. adjective
   c. adverb
   d. interjection

10. <u>Ow!</u> Does my tooth hurt!
    a. noun
    b. conjunction
    c. adjective
    d. interjection

11. Mail your report, <u>or</u> send it by e-mail.
    a. verb
    b. pronoun
    c. conjunction
    d. interjection

12. <u>We</u> plan to go to her home for the holidays.
    a. noun
    b. pronoun
    c. preposition
    d. interjection

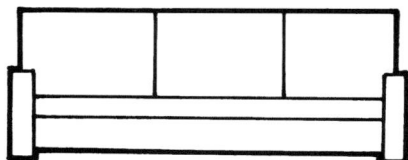

number correct _____
percentage _____

Grammar Test Prep
© The Learning Works, Inc.

Name _____

Parts of Speech Review #3

Directions: What parts of speech are the underlined words in the sentences below?
On the answer sheet, fill in the bubble that corresponds to the correct answer.

1. He was born with a silver spoon in his mouth.
   a. noun – noun
   b. noun – adjective
   c. pronoun – adverb
   d. pronoun – adjective

2. It went in one ear and out the other.
   a. verb – preposition
   b. verb – conjunction
   c. adverb – conjunction
   d. verb – preposition

3. It hit her like a ton of bricks.
   a. pronoun – pronoun
   b. pronoun – noun
   c. verb – adjective
   d. noun – noun

4. They were all in the same boat.
   a. verb – adjective
   b. preposition – adverb
   c. preposition – adjective
   d. pronoun – noun

5. Don't let the cat out of the bag.
   a. verb – noun
   b. adverb – noun
   c. adjective – pronoun
   d. verb – pronoun

6. He has the tiger by the tail.
   a. adjective – noun
   b. interjection – noun
   c. preposition – noun
   d. preposition – pronoun

7. Oh! My sister drives me up the wall.
   a. preposition – noun
   b. interjection – pronoun
   c. pronoun – pronoun
   d. adverb – adjective

8. You have to grab the bull by the horns.
   a. verb – preposition
   b. adverb – verb
   c. verb – conjunction
   d. verb – verb

9. It was so quiet you could hear a pin drop.
   a. adjective – pronoun
   b. adverb – verb
   c. adjective – verb
   d. adverb – noun

10. The answer was right on the tip of my tongue.
    a. adjective – preposition
    b. adverb – preposition
    c. preposition – preposition
    d. noun – interjection

11. You can't have your cake and eat it too.
    a. noun – verb
    b. adverb – noun
    c. pronoun – verb
    d. pronoun – noun

12. You're barking up the wrong tree.
    a. adjective – noun
    b. adjective – adjective
    c. adverb – adjective
    d. verb – adjective

number correct _____
percentage _____

Section 3: Spelling

awkward

bibliography

directory

electricity

gymnasium

intelligence

liability

manufacture

previously

quotation

reflection

scheme

thorough

volunteer

Tricky Words

accede, *verb:* to agree
exceed, *verb:* to surpass

accept, *verb:* to receive
except, *prep.:* other than

adapt, *verb:* to change or adjust
adept, *adj.:* expert, proficient
adopt, *verb:* to receive as one's own

affect, *verb:* to influence
effect, *verb:* to bring about
effect, *noun:* the result

allude, *verb:* to make an indirect reference
elude, *verb:* to dodge or slip away from

ascent, *noun:* the act of going up
assent, *noun:* agreement or approval

beside, *prep.:* next to; by the side of
besides, *prep.:* in addition to

capital, *noun:* a city that is the seat of government
capitol, *noun:* the building in which a legislative body deliberates

complement, *noun:* completing part
compliment, *noun:* an expression of admiration

elicit, *verb:* to bring out or draw forth
illicit, *adj.:* not permitted; unlawful

emigrate, *verb:* to leave one's own country for another
immigrate, *verb:* to come into a country of which one is not a native for permanent residence

former, *adj.:* the first of two
latter, *adj.:* the second of two

lay, *verb:* to place
lie, *verb:* to recline

mania, *noun:* a craze
phobia, *noun:* a fear

persecute, *verb:* to oppress
prosecute, *verb:* to undertake criminal action against

precede, *verb:* to be, come, or go ahead of
proceed, *verb:* to continue after a pause

principal, *adj.:* most important
principal, *noun:* a chief or head woman or man
principle, *noun:* a rule or code of conduct

stationary, *adj.:* 1. not moving. 2. not capable of being moved.
stationery, *noun:* letter paper

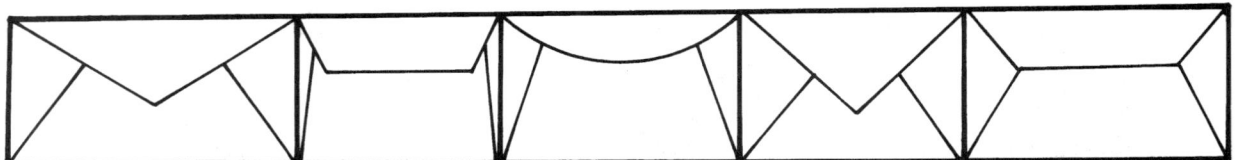

Spelling Plurals #1

Directions: Find the correct spelling of the plural of each word in bold.
On the answer sheet, fill in the bubble that corresponds to the correct answer.

1. **hero**
   a. hero
   b. heros
   c. heroes
   d. herois

2. **journey**
   a. journey
   b. journies
   c. journeys
   d. journeyies

3. **sheep**
   a. sheep
   b. sheeps
   c. sheepies
   d. sheepes

4. **shelf**
   a. shelf
   b. shelfs
   c. shelves
   d. shelfes

5. **mother-in-law**
   a. mother-in-laws
   b. mothers-in-law
   c. mother-in-lawes
   d. mothers-in-laws

6. **lady**
   a. lady
   b. ladys
   c. ladyes
   d. ladies

7. **tragedy**
   a. tragedy
   b. tragedyes
   c. tragedys
   d. tragedies

8. **goose**
   a. goose
   b. gooses
   c. geese
   d. goosies

9. **deer**
   a. deer
   b. deers
   c. deeries
   d. deeres

10. **studio**
    a. studio
    b. studioes
    c. studios
    d. studioss

11. **woman**
    a. woman
    b. womans
    c. women
    d. womens

12. **salmon**
    a. salmon
    b. salmons
    c. salmones
    d. salmonies

number correct _____
percentage _____

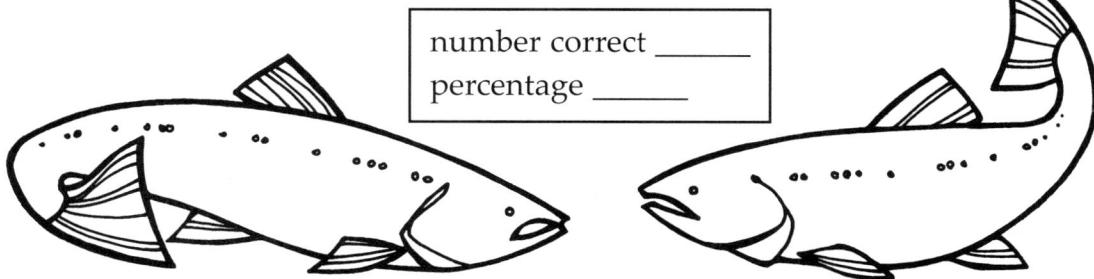

Grammar Test Prep
© The Learning Works, Inc.

Name _____

Spelling Plurals #2

Directions: Find the correct spelling of the plural of each word in bold.
On the answer sheet, fill in the bubble that corresponds to the correct answer.

1. **brush**
   a. brush
   b. brushes
   c. brushies
   d. brushis

2. **ratio**
   a. ratio
   b. ratios
   c. ratioes
   d. ratioss

3. **ox**
   a. ox
   b. oxes
   c. oxs
   d. oxen

4. **chimney**
   a. chimney
   b. chimneys
   c. chimnies
   d. chimneyies

5. **wharf**
   a. wharf
   b. wharfs
   c. wharves
   d. wharfes

6. **larva**
   a. larvas
   b. larvae
   c. larves
   d. larvi

7. **waltz**
   a. waltz
   b. waltzs
   c. waltzes
   d. waltzies

8. **pitch**
   a. pitch
   b. pitches
   c. pitchs
   d. pitchies

9. **alto**
   a. alto
   b. altos
   c. altoes
   d. altoies

10. **veto**
    a. veto
    b. vetos
    c. vetoes
    d. vetoss

11. **embargo**
    a. embargo
    b. embargos
    c. embargoses
    d. embargoes

12. **moose**
    a. moose
    b. mooses
    c. moosies
    d. meese

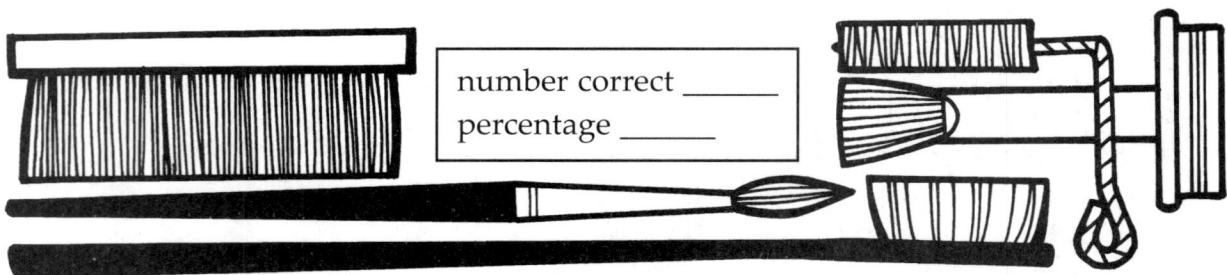

number correct _____
percentage _____

Name _____

Spelling Practice #1

Directions: Find the word that is **not** spelled correctly in each group. On the answer sheet, fill in the bubble that corresponds to the incorrectly spelled word.

1. a. recieve
    b. privilege
    c. foreign
    d. proceeding

2. a. thought
    b. premeum
    c. private
    d. extinguish

3. a. participate
    b. recognize
    c. conseal
    d. liberate

4. a. audience
    b. comittee
    c. formulate
    d. signature

5. a. curiosity
    b. encyclopedia
    c. mispell
    d. identity

6. a. expensive
    b. different
    c. temporary
    d. examenation

7. a. familar
    b. ambitious
    c. increase
    d. minimum

8. a. argument
    b. instrament
    c. yesterday
    d. appointment

9. a. literature
    b. hibernate
    c. mysterous
    d. physical

10. a. session
    b. whimsical
    c. impossable
    d. amazement

11. a. embarass
    b. mosquito
    c. numeral
    d. judgment

12. a. immigrate
    b. seperate
    c. juggle
    d. management

number correct _____
percentage _____

Grammar Test Prep
© The Learning Works, Inc.

Name _____

Spelling Practice #2

Directions: Find the word that is **not** spelled correctly in each group. On the answer sheet, fill in the bubble that corresponds to the incorrectly spelled word.

1. a. conservation
    b. dimension
    c. hemisphere
    d. imposible

2. a. previously
    b. bibliography
    c. scheme
    d. prominant

3. a. ocassion
    b. breakfast
    c. align
    d. quotation

4. a. museum
    b. peculiar
    c. enquiry
    d. anxious

5. a. recognize
    b. innosent
    c. awkward
    d. intelligence

6. a. perticular
    b. tomorrow
    c. assignment
    d. gymnasium

7. a. electricity
    b. similiar
    c. financial
    d. directory

8. a. believe
    b. dominate
    c. scizzors
    d. precious

9. a. genius
    b. liability
    c. quotation
    d. priviledge

10. a. judicial
    b. unbelievable
    c. temperature
    d. reccommend

11. a. investigate
    b. quarrle
    c. formulate
    d. reflection

12. a. supression
    b. thorough
    c. volunteer
    d. manufacture

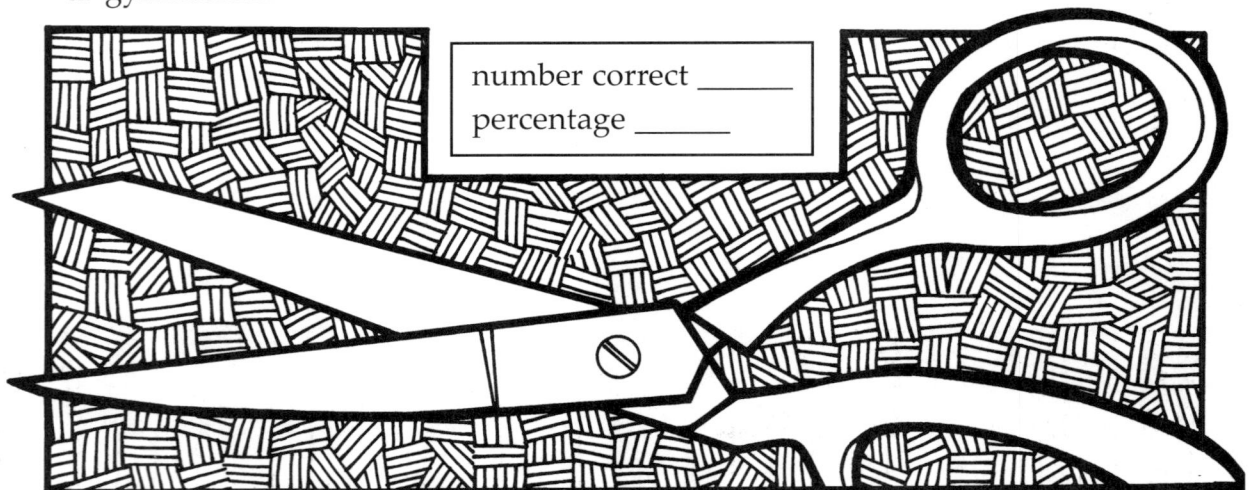

number correct _____
percentage _____

Name _____

Spelling Practice #3

Directions: A word is missing from each sentence below. On the answer sheet,
fill in the bubble next to the word that correctly completes each sentence.

1. She had to _____ for her recital.
   a. practess
   b. praktice
   c. practise
   d. practice

2. The dog ran to _____ the ball.
   a. retreeve
   b. retreive
   c. retrieve
   d. retreve

3. We had to show our _____ at the airport.
   a. identifacation
   b. identification
   c. identificashun
   d. identifecation

4. You'll need your parents' _____ to go.
   a. permision
   b. purmission
   c. permission
   d. purmision

5. She is a _____ member of the community.
   a. prominent
   b. promenent
   c. prominant
   d. prominnet

6. She used a _____ to test the turkey.
   a. thermometor
   b. thermometer
   c. themometer
   d. thermonitor

7. The police officers caught the _____.
   a. theef
   b. theif
   c. thief
   d. thefe

8. The _____ worked on our car.
   a. mechanik
   b. mecanick
   c. machanic
   d. mechanic

9. The teacher had a lot of _____ on his students.
   a. influence
   b. influance
   c. enfluence
   d. influwence

10. The pilot relied on her _____ for the landing.
    a. enstruments
    b. instraments
    c. instrumants
    d. instruments

```
number correct _____
percentage _____
```

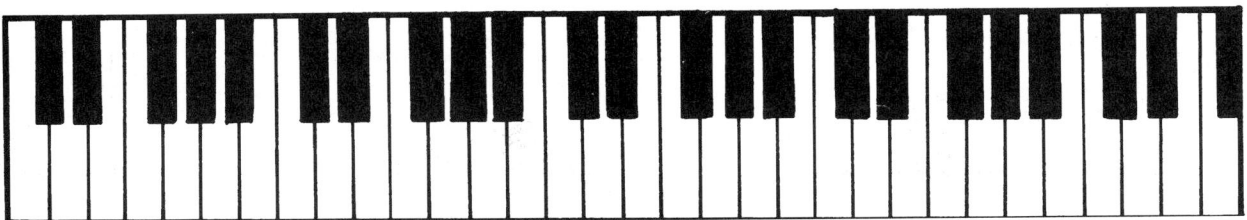

Grammar Test Prep
© The Learning Works, Inc.

Name _____

Spelling Practice #4

Directions: A word is missing from each sentence below.
Fill in the bubble next to the word that correctly completes each sentence.

1. Florida is a _____.
   a. pininsula
   b. peninsula
   c. penninsula
   d. penensula

2. The bank had to _____ his possessions.
   a. seize
   b. seeze
   c. seese
   d. sieze

3. Dad needed a _____ during the operation.
   a. transffusion
   b. transfussion
   c. transfusion
   d. transfushun

4. He was _____ to our needs.
   a. insensitive
   b. ensensative
   c. insensative
   d. incensitive

5. We had to _____ our playoff game.
   a. forfiet
   b. forfeit
   c. forefoot
   d. forfoot

6. Raul wore a clever _____ to the party.
   a. dizguise
   b. disguise
   c. disguize
   d. disguys

7. Did you _____ at the health club today?
   a. exersise
   b. exersize
   c. exercize
   d. exercise

8. I don't like people who are _____.
   a. conceited
   b. konceited
   c. concieted
   d. conceeted

9. We rode the _____ to the third floor.
   a. escalater
   b. esculator
   c. escalator
   d. esscalator

10. She has a good head for _____.
    a. busines
    b. bisness
    c. bizness
    d. business

number correct _____
percentage _____

FUPJXHNDKGREM

Section 4:
Capitalization
and Punctuation

RTQXPJKEIYCNGH

Rules of Capitalization

Before you begin this section of *Grammar Test Prep,*
take time to review the following rules of capitalization:

- Always capitalize the word *I.*

- Capitalize the first word of a sentence or quotation.

- Capitalize abbreviations and titles in names.

    Examples: Dr. Martin Luther King, Jr.
    President Bush

- Capitalize the names of:

people	holidays	nicknames
states	races	ethnic groups
cities	languages	schools
countries	companies and organizations	colleges

- Capitalize words such as *river, street, avenue, park,* etc. when they follow a proper noun.

    Examples: Main Street
    Mississippi River
    Golden Gate Park

- When writing dialog, capitalize the speaker's first word, but not the second part of an interrupted quoted sentence.

    Example: "Of course," she replied, "we plan to attend the play."

- Capitalize the names of historical events and documents.

    Examples: the Civil War
    the Bill of Rights

- Capitalize the names of the days of the week and months.

- Capitalize the main words in the titles of books, poems, movies, television programs, and plays. Words such as *and, the, in,* and *of* are not capitalized unless they are the first word of a title.

- Capitalize the first word of the greeting and first word of the closing of a letter.

- Capitalize words such as north, south, east, and west when they denote regions, but not when they indicate direction.

    Examples: Turn east at the next intersection.
    The Northwest has many severe storms in the winter.

Capitalization Practice #1

Directions: In the following sentences, decide which word or words should be capitalized.
On the answer sheet, fill in the bubble that corresponds to the correct answer.

1. have you read the book *a wrinkle in time*?
    a. Have, Book, Wrinkle
    b. Have, A, Wrinkle, In, Time
    c. Have, Wrinkle, Time
    d. Have, A, Wrinkle, Time

2. mr. smith works for the federal bureau of investigations.
    a. Mr., Smith, Bureau, Investigations
    b. Mr., Smith, Bureau, Of, Investigations
    c. Mr., Smith, Federal, Bureau, Investigations
    d. Mr., Smith, Federal, Bureau, Of, Investigations

3. our class is learning about the milky way in science.
    a. Our, Milky, Way
    b. Our, Milky, Way, Science
    c. Our, Class, Milky, Way
    d. Our, Class, Milky, Way, Science

4. next thursday is thanksgiving, and we are going to boston to celebrate.
    a. Next, Thursday, Boston
    b. Next, Thanksgiving, Boston, Celebrate
    c. Thursday, Thanksgiving, Boston
    d. Next, Thursday, Thanksgiving, Boston

5. the declaration of independence is an important document in american history.
    a. The, Declaration, Independence
    b. The, Declaration, Of, Independence, History
    c. The, Declaration, Independence, American
    d. The, Declaration, Independence, American, History

6. sincerely yours,
    dr. susan h. Nelson (close of a complimentary letter)
    a. Sincerely, Dr., Susan, Nelson
    b. Sincerely, Dr., Susan., H., Nelson
    c. Sincerely, Yours, Susan, H., Nelson
    d. Sincerely, Yours, Dr., Susan, H., Nelson

number correct _____

percentage _____

Name _____

Capitalization Practice #2

Directions: In the following sentences, decide which word or words should be capitalized. On the answer sheet, fill in the bubble that corresponds to the correct answer.

1. "in my opinion," i replied, "she has a great sense of humor."
   a. In, I
   b. In, I, She
   c. In, I, Replied, She
   d. In, Opinion, She, Humor

2. my aunt hannah felt terrible when she dropped and broke mom's favorite china plate.
   a. My, Hannah, China
   b. My, Aunt, Hannah
   c. My, Aunt, Hannah, Mom's
   d. My, Aunt, Hannah, Mom's, China

3. my teacher said that chicago is known as the windy city.
   a. My, Chicago
   b. My, Chicago, Windy, City
   c. My, Teacher, That, Chicago
   d. My, Teacher, Chicago, Windy, City

4. the civil war was a battle between the north and the south that divided many families.
   a. The, Civil, War
   b. The, Civil, North, South
   c. The, Civil, War, North, South
   d. The, Civil, War, Families

5. the congress in washington, d.c., is made up of the senate and the house of representatives.
   a. Congress, Washington, Senate, House
   b. The, Congress, Washington, D.C.
   c. The, Congress, Washington, D.C., Senate, House, Representatives
   d. The, Congress, Washington, D.C., Senate, House, Of, Representatives

6. steve asked, "do you have my copy of *newsweek*, mike?"
   a. Steve, Newsweek, Mike
   b. Steve, Do, Newsweek
   c. Steve, Do, Mike
   d. Steve, Do, Newsweek, Mike

number correct _____
percentage _____

★★★★★★★★★★★★★★★★★★

Name _____

Capitalization Practice #3

Directions: In the following sentences, decide which word or words should be capitalized. On the answer sheet, fill in the bubble that corresponds to the correct answer.

1. the jones family headed west on their vacation to utah last summer.
   a. The, Jones, West
   b. The, Jones, West, Utah
   c. The, Jones, Utah
   d. The, Jones, West, Utah, Summer

2. on thursday, we are going to begin studying the constitution in my history class.
   a. On, Constitution
   b. On, Thursday, History
   c. On, Thursday
   d. On, Thursday, Constitution

3. "have you read *the iliad* by homer?" asked professor nelson.
   a. "Have, Iliad, Professor, Nelson
   b. Have, The, Iliad, Professor, Nelson
   c. Have, The, Iliad, Homer, Professor, Nelson
   d. Have, Iliad, Professor, Nelson

4. her birthday is may 3, and we plan to take her to the theater to see "the lion king."
   a. Her, May, The, Lion, King
   b. Her, Birthday, Theater, Lion, King
   c. Her, May, Lion, King
   d. Her, May, Theater, King

5. the chinese ambassador arrived at john f. kennedy airport this week.
   a. The, Chinese, John, F., Kennedy, Airport
   b. The, Chinese, Ambassador, John., F., Kennedy
   c. The, John, F., Kennedy
   d. The, Chinese, Ambassador, John, F., Kennedy, Airport

6. the supreme court in washington, d.c., is the highest court in the united states.
   a. The, Supreme, Washington, D.C.
   b. The, Supreme, Court, Washington
   c. The, Court, Washington, D.C., Court, United, States
   d. The, Supreme, Court, Washington, D.C., United, States

number correct _____

percentage _____

45

Rules of Punctuation

Before you begin this section of *Grammar Test Prep,*
take time to review the following rules of punctuation:

Periods

- Use a period at the end of a sentence that is a statement or a command.

- Use a period after initials in names and after most abbreviations.

Commas

- Use a comma to separate the day of the month from the year. Also use a comma to separate the year from the rest of the sentence.

- Use a comma to separate the name of a city from a state or country. Also use a comma to set off a state or country from the rest of the sentence.

- Use a comma to set off the name of a person being spoken to.

- Use a comma to separate words in a series.

- Use a comma to set off "yes" or "no" at the beginning of a sentence.

- Use a comma before a conjunction (such as "and," "but," "or," "yet," and "nor") when it joins two independent clauses.

    Example: We wanted to go to the soccer game, but Dad couldn't get the car started.

- Use a comma to separate a subordinate clause at the beginning of a sentence from the main clause.

    Example: After the movie, we all went out for dessert.

- Use a comma between a quotation and the rest of the sentence, unless a question mark or exclamation point is needed.

- Use a comma after the greeting and after the closing of a friendly letter.

Question Marks

- Use a question mark at the end of a sentence that asks a question.

Exclamation Points

- Use an exclamation point at the end of a sentence or quotation that shows strong feelings.

Rules of Punctuation
(continued)

Quotation Marks

- Use quotation marks before and after words used in a direct quotation.
- Use quotation marks around the titles of stories, poems, speeches, songs, and television programs.

Apostrophes

- Use an apostrophe to show where letters have been left out of a contraction.
- Add an apostrophe and "s" to singular nouns to show possession or ownership.
- Add an apostrophe to plural nouns ending in "s" to show possession or ownership.

Colons

- Use a colon after the greeting of a business letter.
- Use a colon at the beginning of a list of things in a sentence.
- Use a colon to separate hours and minutes when writing times.

Semicolons

- Use a semicolon in a compound sentence between two independent clauses that are not joined by a conjunction.
- Use a semicolon before the words "however" and "therefore" when they are used to join clauses in a compound sentence.

Hyphens

- Use a hyphen to divide a word into syllables for spelling or pronunciation purposes.
- Use a hyphen at the end of a line when a word is broken and is continued on the next line.
- Use a hyphen between the parts of a compound word.

Parentheses

- Use parentheses to enclose parts of a sentence that could be left out, such as explanations or comments.

Name _____

Punctuation Practice #1

Directions: In each sentence, find the correct punctuation mark that is needed. On the answer sheet, fill in the bubble that corresponds to the correct answer.

1. Mr Gordon was a guest speaker in our class today.
   a. .
   b. "
   c. ,
   d. ?

2. "Do you know how to ski" asked Megan.
   a. .
   b. ,
   c. ?
   d. "

3. I hope you can go to the movies with me," said Mike.
   a. !
   b. ?
   c. "
   d. '

4. Watch out for that fire
   a. .
   b. "
   c. ?
   d. !

5. I take piano lessons on Tuesdays and Thursdays
   a. .
   b. "
   c. !
   d. ,

6. I bought pencils paper, and erasers at the store.
   a. .
   b. ,
   c. "
   d. '

7. My favorite foods are pizza chicken and hamburgers.
   a. !
   b. ,
   c. "
   d. ?

8. Wow, that was a fantastic concert
   a. "
   b. ,
   c. !
   d. ?

9. My mother is wearing my grand-mothers ring.
   a. .
   b. !
   c. '
   d.)

10. Dad was born in Dayton Ohio.
    a. !
    b. ,
    c. "
    d. .

11. Vicki said, "I'm enjoying this book.
    a. "
    b. ,
    c. ;
    d. ?

12. The dog wagged its tail when it saw me
    a. ,
    b. "
    c. '
    d. .

number correct _____
percentage _____

Name _____

Punctuation Practice #2

Directions: Find the sentence that has correct punctuation. On the answer sheet, fill in the bubble that corresponds to the correct answer. Then, on a separate piece of paper, correct the punctuation mistakes in the other three sentences in each group.

1. a. The cat licked it's whiskers after eating dinner.
   b. I bought lettuce, tomatoes, and bread at the grocery store.
   c. Jenny asked, "Have you bought any new baseball cards for your collection."
   d. No we can't join you for a movie tonight, but maybe we can go tomorrow.

2. a. "Is this Katherines desk?" inquired Mr. R J Morrell.
   b. I enjoyed reading Dr Martin Luther Kings I Have a Dream speech.
   c. Let's play video games; its too hot to play outside.
   d. Although it's very early in the morning, let's get started on our road trip.

3. a. Dad ordered fish but Mom wanted to order a steak.
   b. I believe in physical fitness so I try to run at least three times a week.
   c. Zoe's project was due by 3:00 on Friday.
   d. "Thats the best ice hockey game I've ever seen," exclaimed Yolanda!

4. a. My grandmother was born in Miami, Florida but she hasnt been back there in years.
   b. No that's not a good time for me to meet you.
   c. "I'll take you to the bowling alley," Dad said, "but let me finish my crossword puzzle."
   d. "Ouch," he cried. "A bee just stung me on my neck!"

5. a. "Is that phone call for me?" Kevin shouted from the top of the stairs.
   b. "Leslie," Mom asked, "where did you put my scissors."
   c. My sisters birthday is on Valentines' Day.
   d. "Matthew would you please turn that stereo down? she asked.

6. a. A fierce violent storm is expected to hit the coast by 5:00.
   b. Delicious smell's came from the kitchen as Dad cooked his famous spaghetti sauce.
   c. She's the class president; therefore, she's expected to give a speech at graduation.
   d. I need the following items from the hardware store, nails, screws, and a hammer.

number correct _____
percentage _____

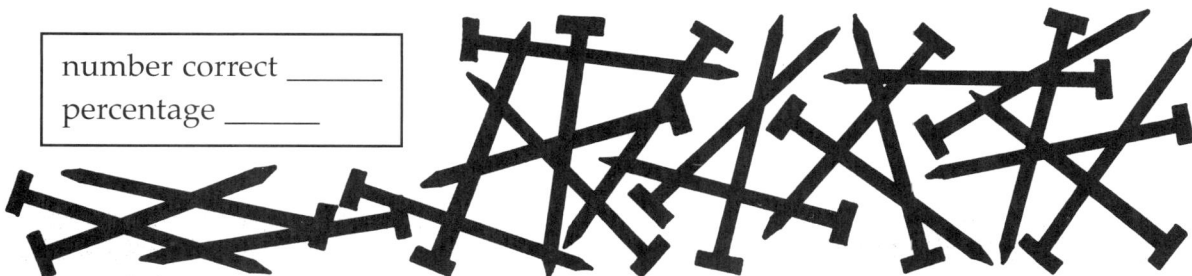

Grammar Test Prep
© The Learning Works, Inc.

Name _____

Punctuation Practice #3

Directions: Find the sentence that has correct punctuation. On the answer sheet, fill in the bubble that corresponds to the correct answer. Then, on a separate piece of paper, correct the punctuation mistakes in the other three sentences in each group.

1. a. "Did you find out what time the movie starts." asked Vicki.
   b. We are planning a trip to Washington, D.C, next summer.
   c. Jasons father is a famous composer.
   d. This view of the Grand Canyon is absolutely incredible!

2. a. I wonder if our team will make it to the finals?
   b. By recycling our newspapers, we can cut down on trash in our landfills.
   c. My family plans to come to Parent's Night at school, and see my work that's on display.
   d. The director, Mrs. Michaels asked me to come back for a second audition.

3. a. "What do you want me to bring," Greg asked.
   b. When it's my turn to pick a movie, I want to see an adventure film.
   c. Marty said, You can be on my team every year!"
   d. There were red blue, green, and yellow balloons at the festival.

4. a. When you finish your essay read it over to check for spelling and punctuation errors.
   b. Malcolm, an outstanding basketball player was presented with a trophy last night.
   c. Bill asked Lori if she had seen his car keys anywhere around the house?
   d. On September 25, 2001, the new stadium will open in St. Louis, Missouri.

5. a. "Wow," he exclaimed, "this pan is really hot."
   b. The worlds population is growing at an alarming rate.
   c. Our new house was completed this week; it took more than two years to build.
   d. I received thirty five cents change from my purchase.

6. a. Captain T R. Hawkins was awarded a medal for his military service.
   b. "The tree in our backyard loses it's leaves every winter," she said.
   c. You can do one of three things; go now, go later, or don't go at all.
   d. Oh, no! I left my camera at home!

number correct _____
percentage _____

Final Review

Read each sentence on this page and page 52.
Find and count the mistakes you find in usage, grammar,
spelling, punctuation, and capitalization. On the answer sheet,
fill in the bubble that corresponds to the correct answer.

1. If you went to the pharmacy this afternoon, will you buy me two boxes of cough drops.
   a. 2
   b. 3
   c. 4
   d. 5

2. The line for the movie was to long so we decide to leave and come back later," said dr Presser.
   a. 4
   b. 5
   c. 6
   d. 7

3. I beleive their is going to be troubel because everybody seems on edge?
   a. 4
   b. 5
   c. 6
   d. 7

4. "The school store sold the following item on friday; penciles, pennants, and sweat-shirts," reported Katherine
   a. 4
   b. 5
   c. 6
   d. 7

5. The childrens' crys could be herd all over the playground.
   a. 3
   b. 4
   c. 5
   d. 6

6. "Lie the cake on the kitchin counter," requested Mrs Thomas.
   a. 3
   b. 4
   c. 5
   d. 6

number correct _____
percentage _____

Final Review
(continued)

7. Jack said, Everyone in are family like french food."
   a. 3
   b. 4
   c. 5
   d. 6

8. "Labor day is allways celebrated on the first monday in Septembor, said Pedro
   a. 4
   b. 5
   c. 6
   d. 7

9. He done me a tremendous favor; he mow my overrgrown lawn.
   a. 2
   b. 3
   c. 4
   d. 5

10. "Their are to many people crowd on the busses," stated Mr Levy.
    a. 4
    b. 5
    c. 6
    d. 7

11. After the rehearsal all of the kid's are gone to get pizza.
    a. 3
    b. 4
    c. 5
    d. 6

12. Randy is the tallest of the two: hes' allmost six foot tall.
    a. 4
    b. 5
    c. 6
    d. 7

number correct _____
percentage _____

Answer Key

Page 11 • Usage – Practice #1

1.	c	7.	b
2.	a	8.	d
3.	d	9.	d
4.	c	10.	a
5.	d	11.	c
6.	a	12.	b

Page 12 • Usage – Practice #2

1.	d	7.	b
2.	b	8.	d
3.	c	9.	a
4.	d	10.	d
5.	c	11.	b
6.	a	12.	b

Page 13 • Usage – Practice #3

1.	b	7.	c
2.	b	8.	b
3.	d	9.	c
4.	a	10.	a
5.	d	11.	d
6.	c	12.	a

Page 14 • Usage – Practice #4

1.	c	7.	d
2.	b	8.	a
3.	c	9.	c
4.	a	10.	b
5.	d	11.	c
6.	b	12.	d

Page 15 • Usage – Practice #5

1.	d	7.	a
2.	a	8.	a
3.	b	9.	b
4.	c	10.	b
5.	a	11.	d
6.	d	12.	c

Page 16 • Usage – Practice #6

1.	b	7.	d
2.	c	8.	d
3.	a	9.	b
4.	c	10.	c
5.	b	11.	a
6.	c	12.	b

Page 17 • Usage – Practice #7

1.	b	7.	b
2.	c	8.	d
3.	a	9.	c
4.	d	10.	d
5.	c	11.	a
6.	a	12.	b

Page 18 • Usage – Practice #8

1.	c	7.	d
2.	b	8.	c
3.	c	9.	d
4.	b	10.	a
5.	c	11.	b
6.	b	12.	c

Page 20 • Nouns

1.	b	7.	c
2.	d	8.	a
3.	c	9.	d
4.	d	10.	c
5.	a	11.	b
6.	c	12.	d

Page 21 • Pronouns

1.	c	7.	a
2.	b	8.	c
3.	d	9.	b
4.	a	10.	d
5.	d	11.	a
6.	b	12.	b

Page 22 • Verbs

1.	d	6.	d
2.	c	7.	b
3.	c	8.	b
4.	a	9.	c
5.	c	10.	b

Page 23 • Review of Nouns, Pronouns, and Verbs

1.	c	4.	d
2.	d	5.	a
3.	b	6.	b

Page 25 • Subject–Verb Agreement

1.	a	4.	a
2.	c	5.	d
3.	c	6.	c

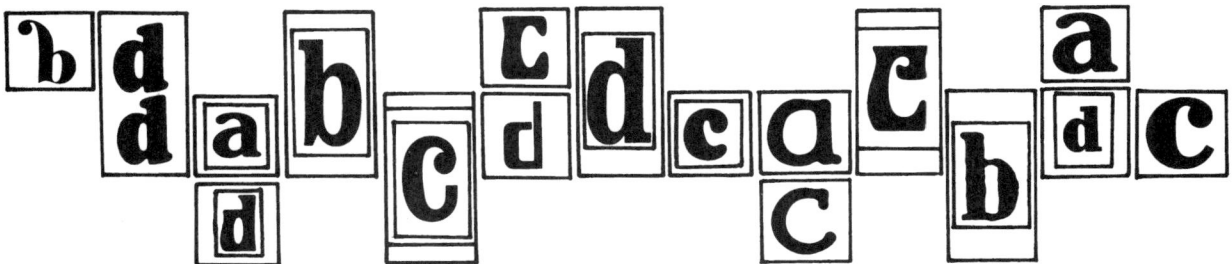

Answer Key
(continued)

Page 26 • Adjectives

1.	b	7.	a
2.	d	8.	c
3.	c	9.	d
4.	a	10.	c
5.	b	11.	d
6.	d	12.	a

Page 27 • Adverbs

1.	b	4.	c
2.	d	5.	a
3.	d	6.	c

Page 28 • Parts of Speech Review #1

1.	c	7.	c
2.	d	8.	b
3.	d	9.	c
4.	a	10.	d
5.	a	11.	c
6.	b	12.	b

Page 29 • Prepositions

1.	c	4.	b
2.	d	5.	a
3.	a		

Page 30 • Conjunctions and Interjections

1.	b	6.	b
2.	c	7.	d
3.	a	8.	a
4.	d	9.	b
5.	b	10.	d

Page 31 • Parts of Speech Review #2

1.	c	7.	a
2.	d	8.	b
3.	c	9.	c
4.	b	10.	d
5.	c	11.	c
6.	a	12.	b

Page 32 • Parts of Speech Review #3

1.	d	7.	b
2.	b	8.	d
3.	a	9.	c
4.	c	10.	b
5.	a	11.	c
6.	c	12.	d

Page 35 • Spelling Plurals #1

1.	c	7.	d
2.	c	8.	c
3.	a	9.	a
4.	c	10.	c
5.	b	11.	c
6.	d	12.	a

Page 36 • Spelling Plurals #2

1.	b	7.	c
2.	b	8.	b
3.	d	9.	b
4.	b	10.	c
5.	c	11.	d
6.	b	12.	a

Page 37 • Spelling Practice #1

1.	a	7.	a
2.	b	8.	b
3.	c	9.	c
4.	b	10.	c
5.	c	11.	a
6.	d	12.	b

Page 38 • Spelling Practice #2

1.	d	7.	b
2.	d	8.	c
3.	a	9.	d
4.	c	10.	d
5.	b	11.	b
6.	a	12.	a

Page 39 • Spelling Practice #3

1.	d	6.	b
2.	c	7.	c
3.	b	8.	d
4.	c	9.	a
5.	a	10.	d

Page 40 • Spelling Practice #4

1.	b	6.	b
2.	a	7.	d
3.	c	8.	a
4.	a	9.	c
5.	b	10.	d

Page 43 • Capitalization Practice #1

1.	d	4.	d
2.	c	5.	c
3.	a	6.	b

Page 44 • Capitalization Practice #2

1.	a	4.	c
2.	c	5.	c
3.	b	6.	d

Page 45 • Capitalization Practice #3

1.	c	4.	a
2.	d	5.	a
3.	c	6.	d

Page 48 • Punctuation Practice #1

1.	a	7.	b
2.	c	8.	c
3.	c	9.	c
4.	d	10.	b
5.	a	11.	a
6.	b	12.	d

Answer Key

(continued)

Page 49 • Punctuation Practice #2

1. a. The cat licked <u>its</u> whiskers after eating dinner.
    b. correct
    c. Jenny asked, "Have you bought any new baseball cards for your collection<u>?</u>"
    d. No<u>,</u> we can't join you for a movie tonight, but maybe we can go tomorrow.

2. a. "Is this Katherine<u>'</u>s desk?" inquired Mr. R<u>.</u> J<u>.</u> Morrell.
    b. I enjoyed reading Dr<u>.</u> Martin Luther King<u>'</u>s <u>"</u>I Have a Dream<u>"</u> speech.
    c. Let's play video games; it<u>'</u>s too hot to play outside.
    d. correct

3. a. Dad ordered fish<u>,</u> but Mom wanted to order a steak.
    b. I believe in physical fitness<u>,</u> so I try to run at least three times a week.
    c. correct
    d. "That<u>'</u>s the best ice hockey game I've ever seen!" exclaimed Yolanda<u>.</u>

4. a. My grandmother was born in Miami, Florida<u>,</u> but she hasn<u>'</u>t been back there in years.
    b. No<u>,</u> that's not a good time for me to meet you.
    c. correct
    d. "Ouch<u>!</u>" he cried. "A bee just stung me on my neck!"

5. **a. correct**
    b. "Leslie," Mom asked, "where did you put my scissors<u>?</u>"
    c. My sister<u>'</u>s birthday is on Valentine<u>'</u>s Day.
    d. "Matthew<u>,</u> would you please turn that stereo down?<u>"</u> she asked.

6. a. A fierce<u>,</u> violent storm is expected to hit the coast by 5:00.
    b. Delicious smell<u>s</u> came from the kitchen as Dad cooked his famous spaghetti sauce.
    c. correct
    d. I need the following items from the hardware store<u>:</u> nails, screws, and a hammer.

55

Grammar Test Prep
© The Learning Works, Inc.

Answer Key

(continued)

Page 50 • Punctuation Practice #3

1. a. "Did you find out what time the movie starts<u>?</u>" asked Vicki.
    b. We are planning a trip to Washington, D.C<u>.</u>, next summer.
    c. Jason<u>'s</u> father is a famous composer.
    d. correct

2. a. I wonder if our team will make it to the finals<u>.</u>
    b. correct
    c. My family plans to come to Parent<u>s'</u> Night at school, and see my work that's on display.
    d. The director, Mrs. Michaels<u>,</u> asked me to come back for a second audition.

3. a. "What do you want me to bring<u>?</u>" Greg asked.
    b. correct
    c. Marty said, <u>"</u>You can be on my team every year!"
    d. There were red<u>,</u> blue, green, and yellow balloons at the festival.

4. a. When you finish your essay<u>,</u> read it over to check for spelling and punctuation errors.
    b. Malcolm, an outstanding basketball player<u>,</u> was presented with a trophy last night.
    c. Bill asked Lori if she had seen his car keys anywhere around the house<u>.</u>
    d. correct

5. a. "Wow<u>!</u>" he exclaimed<u>.</u> "<u>t</u>his pan is really hot."
    b. The world<u>'s</u> population is growing at an alarming rate.
    c. correct
    d. I received thirty<u>-</u>five cents change from my purchase.

6. a. Captain T<u>.</u> R. Hawkins was awarded a medal for his military service.
    b. "The tree in our backyard loses <u>its</u> leaves every winter," she said.
    c. You can do one of three things<u>:</u> go now, go later, or don't go at all.
    d. correct

Pages 51–52 • Final Review (The total number of mistakes appears in bold type.)

1. If you g<u>o</u> to the pharmacy this afternoon, will you buy me two boxes of cough drops<u>?</u> **(a: 2)**

2. <u>"</u>The line for the movie was <u>too</u> long<u>,</u> so we <u>decided</u> to leave and come back later," said <u>Dr.</u> Presser. **(c: 6)**

3. I <u>believe</u> <u>there</u> is going to be <u>trouble</u><u>,</u> because everybody seems on edge<u>.</u> **(b: 5)**

4. "The school store sold the following <u>items</u> on <u>F</u>riday<u>:</u> <u>pencils</u>, pennants, and sweatshirts," reported Katherine<u>.</u> **(b: 5)**

5. The <u>children's</u> <u>cries</u> could be <u>heard</u> all over the playground. **(a: 3)**

6. "<u>Lay</u> the cake on the <u>kitchen</u> counter," requested Mrs<u>.</u> Thomas. **(a: 3)**

7. Jack said, <u>"</u>Everyone in <u>our</u> family <u>likes</u> <u>F</u>rench food." **(b: 4)**

8. "Labor <u>Day</u> is <u>always</u> celebrated on the first <u>Monday</u> in <u>September</u><u>,</u>" said Pedro<u>.</u> **(c: 6)**

9. He <u>did</u> me a tremendous favor; he <u>mowed</u> my <u>overgrown</u> lawn. **(b: 3)**

10. "<u>There</u> are <u>too</u> many people <u>crowded</u> on the <u>buses</u>," stated Mr<u>.</u> Levy. **(b: 5)**

11. After the rehearsal<u>,</u> all of the <u>kids</u> are <u>going</u> to get pizza. **(a: 3)**

12. Randy is the <u>taller</u> of the two<u>;</u> <u>he's</u> <u>almost</u> six <u>feet</u> tall. **(b: 5)**

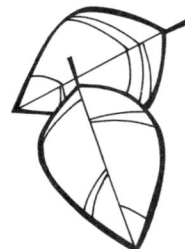

Grammar Test Prep
© The Learning Works, Inc.

56